Old Mauchline
Ian Lyell

With important roads from Ayr to Edinburgh and Kilmarnock to Dumfries crossing at this point, it was inevitable that Mauchline would be established and grow around the junction. We are told in *Rambles Through the Land of Burns* that in the early nineteenth century, 'In the centre of the square stood a curious pillar-shaped erection, which served both as a gas lamp and a water pump, supplying light above and water below. There was also a wooden erection from which was suspended a pair of scales and in these all the butter and wool and other commodities sold at the market were weighed and a duty laid on them'. In 1820 a new road was driven through from north to south, replacing the Back Causey, Castle Street and the Cowgate. This involved the demolition of a property belonging to Burns's friend James Smith and, opposite it, the Sun Inn belonging to the Miller family. J. Lambie was a merchant and church elder who apparently enjoyed enquiring into the morals of the townsfolk. The smoke is coming from a chimney at Smith's boxware factory.

Text © Ian Lyell, 2020.
First published in the United Kingdom, 2020,
by Stenlake Publishing Ltd,
54-58 Mill Square,
Catrine, Ayrshire,
KA5 6RD

Telephone: 01290 551122
www.stenlake.co.uk

Printed by P2D,
1 Newlands Road,
Westoning,
MK45 5LD

ISBN 9781840338683

The publishers regret that they cannot supply copies of any pictures featured in this book.

Acknowledgements

Particular thanks to Kenny Baird for access to his website ayrshirehistory.com, without which this book would not have been possible.

Picture Acknowledgements

Alex Devaney: page 19
Alistair Milne: pages 7, 12
Betty McCartney: page 11
Burns House Museum: pages 8, 15, 20, 23, 29, 31, 37, 41
Guy Howie: pages 32, 33
Hugh Hodge: page 25
Ian Lyell: pages 17 (lower), 48
Jimmy Davidson: page 49 (left)

John Halliday: page 52
Mrs Terry: page 16 and inside back cover
Pat Alexander: inside front cover
Richard Stenlake: page 27
Scott Wallace: page 35
Terry Harrison: pages 13, 18, 26

William Lyle: front cover, back cover and pages 1, 4, 5, 6, 9, 10, 14, 17 (upper), 21, 22, 24, 28, 30, 34, 36, 38, 39, 40, 42, 43, 44, 45, 46, 47, 49 (right), 50, 51, 53, 54, 55, 56

Further Reading

The books listed below were used by the author during his research. None of them is available from Stenlake Publishing. Those interested in finding out more are advised to contact their local bookshop or reference library.

Archibald Armstrong, *Rambles Through the Land of Burns*, 1879.
W.F. Blair, *An Octogenarian's Reminiscences, Kilmarnock Standard*, 1922.
J.T. Gibb, *Mauchline Town and District*, 1911.
Mrs Nathaniel Hawthorne, *Notes in England and Italy*, 1861.
John Hood, *Old Mauchline and Tarbolton*, 2001.
T. Killen, *Guide to Mauchline Catrine and Sorn*, 1909.
Dane Love, *History of Mauchline Village and Parish*, 2012.
I. Lyell, *Mauchline in Times Past*, 1986.

I. Lyell, *The Mauchline Burns Club 90th Anniversary*, 2013.
Dr. D Rawson, *Ballochmyle Jubilee*, 1990.
H. Steven, *Mauchline Its History and Associations*, 1897.
J. Strawhorn, *Mauchline Memories of Robert Burns*, 1985.
Mauchline, Historic Scotland, 2006.
Ayr Advertiser, 1893.
First Statistical Account of Scotland.
Interview with Miss Hyslop, 1971.

Introduction

Of Celtic origin, the name Mauchline literally means a place of water, deriving from *magh* – grass or field – and *lyn* – water or stream. The earliest sign of civilisation in the area is the Neolithic or Bronze Age cup-and-ring-marked rock near Ballochmyle Bridge, two kilometres from Mauchline. It has been suggested that the long straight stretch of modern road to the north of Mauchline follows the course of a Roman one, but while excavations have revealed traces of earlier roads, a Roman date has not been confirmed. It is known that in 787 an army of Cruthni (or Cruthin), invaders from Ireland, was defeated by local people on a moor near Mauchline, possibly the site of the cemetery on Barskimming Road.

Mauchline first appears securely in the history records early in the reign of William I, The Lion (1165–1214), when a grant of the land of Mauchline was made to Melrose Abbey. In 1243 a monk was appointed to manage the abbey's affairs there and the settlement was an agrarian grange rather than an actual monastery. In 1315 the Bishop of Glasgow allowed Melrose Abbey to raise a parochial church, which remained in use even after the Reformation and until its replacement in 1829. Around 1450 Abbot Hunter built a tower to serve as a civil residence to manage the Mauchline estate. This building is still standing and is known today as the A-listed Castle.

In 1510 Mauchline became a burgh of barony with the privilege of holding a weekly Wednesday market. By this time the village had a saddler, smith, potter, mason and nine innkeepers. It can be safely assumed that the Cross was the site of the market. In 1544 Protestant preacher George Wishart was barred entry into the church by local Catholic gentry; however, religious allegiances changed over the next fifty years and John Knox preached there in 1599.

There is some evidence that a school existed by at least the 1640s. The Covenanting movement was well supported in Mauchline, with the minister signing the National Covenant in 1648. That same year a large communion was attended by hundreds of people and the Battle of Mauchline Moor also took place between Covenanting and Royalist forces. In 1669 troops were quartered in the village and continued as a presence until the 1680s. 1685 witnessed the hanging of five Covenanters.

In 1707 the burgh was made a burgh of regality in favour of the Earl of Loudon. Around the same time Poosie Nansie's Inn opened, later to be the scene of Burns's 'Jolly Beggars'. By 1755 the population of Mauchline was 1,200 and in 1756 the property 'The Place' was built at the Cross for ladies of the house of Eglinton (it was demolished around 1930). The grounds of this substantial mansion stretched up High Street.

A local leather industry thrived with the still extant Tanfield Lane testimony to this. Developing industries were wide ranging: hand-loom weaving was being replaced by fancy wood work, known today as the highly collectable Mauchline Ware, while sandstone quarrying, a creamery, and a curling stone factory appeared along with many shoe makers.

In February 1784 Robert Burns leased and moved into Mossgiel Farm. Two years later the poet published his 'Kilmarnock Edition' of poems which were written at the farm and were largely inspired by Mauchline's people and activities. In 1789 the school was removed from the church and opened in Mansefield Road. By 1791 the population was recorded as 1,800.

In 1826 a new street plan was superimposed on the old, with the opening of wider and straighter streets including New Road and Earl Grey Street. Buildings at the north and south ends of the Cross were demolished to allow this new pattern. Around this time the sandstone quarries were also beginning to transform the streets as many older buildings were gradually demolished and replaced.

Mauchline Parish Church was built in 1829 from a design by local architect William Alexander. The manufacture of wooden boxes was by then the most notable industry, there being three sites for this. Among them was the business of W. & A. Smith, in business between 1810 and 1937. Curling stones were also being manufactured by this time and their production survives today as a unique and important industry for Mauchline. Coal mining was carried out at the local Mauchline Colliery and the village had its own gas works. By 1837 there was a post office, four schools, a prison with two cells, two inns, fifteen ale houses and a public library.

Writing in 1859 while on a Burns pilgrimage, Mrs Nathaniel Hawthorne (wife of the American author Nathaniel Hawthorne) described the village as 'looking rusty and timeworn', with 'wretched little dwellings'. In 1831 the population of Mauchline was recorded as 1,364, a reduction from the 1791 figure although by 1881 the numbers had recovered to 1,616. 1897 saw the opening of the National Burns Memorial Tower, designed by William Fraser, while the 1930s saw the building of council houses to the north of the town along with a series of bungalows along Cumnock Road. Council housing continued post 1945 in the Welton Farm area. Since the 1980s considerable private housing has been built at the Ayr and Catrine exits.

In 2003 the Mauchline Burns Club initiated an annual Holy Fair which has attracted annually over 10,000 visitors. The club has also been responsible for several enhancing features in the village, among them a Jean Armour statue, blue plaques and guides of significant sites and graves, and pavement plaques on Burns-related themes. The Burns House Museum, now owned by East Ayrshire Council, offers displays on Burns, curling stones and Mauchline ware. Today there is relatively little industry remaining in the town other than the curling stone factory. The most recent population estimate, from 2015, indicates a population of 4,030.

Mauchline remains a town with a very varied past, which to this day is reflected in its street layout and its buildings which range in age from the medieval to the twentieth century. In 2019 the Mauchline Burns Club, supported by East Ayrshire Council, was successful in its submission of a Conservation Area Regeneration Scheme project to Historic Environment Scotland, which resulted in an award of over £2million for the upgrading and refurbishment of buildings in the village centre. The Cross has always been the hub of the village, and with this in mind, these pages have been arranged moving from the Cross to the north, south, east and west, always returning to the Cross.

Left: Castle Street is the site of the Burns House Museum complex and was once the main entrance to Mauchline from the north. In 1788 Burns and Jean Armour began their formalised married life in the upper floor of the building where the sign is, before moving to Ellisland, Dumfriesshire, later that year. In 1915 Charles Rennie Cowie of Glasgow sponsored the renovation of the property, allowing it to open as a museum on the top floor with accommodation for elderly ladies on the ground floor. Due to poor amenities, the occupants were moved in 1959 to modern cottages adjacent to Mossgiel Farm. Further development took place in 1967–69, again in the 1990s, and in 2003 when ownership of the building was sold to East Ayrshire Council. The building opposite was Nanse Tinnock's ale house, where Burns, a frequent visitor, read manuscripts of his poems to an eager audience.

Further along Castle Street from Burns's house is the area known as The Knowe. None of the buildings seen here exist today; after their demolition in the mid 1800s the site remained empty until the 1960s when a private house was built facing and a council block on the right. The man on the right is John Reid, a mason by trade. Behind him was the site of the Elbow Tavern (not seen in the picture), belonging to an old sailor known as 'the old tar'. Here, Burns had secret meetings with Mary Campbell, also known as Highland Mary. The building, soon in a state of poor repair, became a cattle shelter. Further to the left but out of view stood Brownlea House, home of Burns's Mary Morrison, and opposite was another group of houses known as 'Clinkum Square'. One of the occupants, Clinkumbell, was the town crier in Burns's day.

The anti-burgher kirk was built in 1796 with considerable difficulty. The anti-burghers were against the local landowners choosing their minister over themselves and, due to these religious differences, the builders were refused access to a local quarry. However, stones were carried from supportive farms, as well being excavated from the ground within the four walls of the church during construction. It had an outside stair and held 600 worshippers. In its latter days congregants had to be very careful as 'on one or two occasions an unwary step led to the floor and ceiling underneath being pierced with somewhat ludicrous results'. In 1884 it was replaced on the same site by the Walker Memorial Free Church in memory of the first minister of 1796. The memorial stone of the original church is now to be found at the entrance of the parish church. It had come from the hearth of an old Catrine widow who had been unable to make a financial contribution.

In 1925 the congregation of the Walker Memorial Church, on The Knowe and seen here, united with that of the Abbey Church, Loudoun Street, on the latter's closure. In 1929 it became the North Church and in 1976 the congregation united with that of the parish church, with that church's Very Rev. Dr. Morrice becoming the first minister of the combined congregations which continued as Mauchline Parish Church. In 1983 the empty North Church building was demolished and a private house was built on the site. The church hall on the right also became a private residence.

Built in 1880, the Temperance Hall on Kilmarnock Road stood on the site of the present-day Hospice Charity Shop. It was built in 1870, probably with the involvement of the Mauchline Total Abstinence Society, and as a community hall it replaced the use of farm barns for local 'kirns' – country dances. The 'large hall', which was on the street level, held 500 people, while downstairs the 'lesser hall' served partly as a public library which in 1919 boasted 2,000 books paid for by subscriptions, supplemented by regularly changing volumes supplied by the council. In 1896 a concert was held here to commemorate the laying of the foundation stone of the National Burns Memorial and in 1923 it was also the place where sixteen gentlemen met to form the Mauchline Burns Club, which is still in existence. Lantern-slide lectures were held in the hall in winter, with the speaker often having to stay overnight because of the lack of transport. On the occasion of the annual flower show the hall hosted the many entries for baking and handicrafts competitions. It was demolished on safety grounds in 1965.

The post office in Mauchline occupied many sites through the years. This photograph was taken at the Kilmarnock Road premises prior to its move in 1905 to a new site at the corner of Loudoun Street and Barskimming Road in 'premises specially designed for its requirements'. Those gathered here, office staff and postmen, include the head postmistress Miss Miller. The horse was called Mick and seen behind his head is a boyish Willie McFarlane, who later became post master and parish church session clerk. On the departure of the post office, the building was occupied by Simon Currie's fish and chip shop and then in 1930 by the Italian Vanni family who opened their Castle Cafe. The premises were extended into the gap on the right for use as a restaurant. This closed in 1960 and is now a solicitors' office, although the Vannis still own the café.

This overview of New Road (renamed Kilmarnock Road in 1970) was taken from the church tower. Bottom right is the Temperance Hall; the gap opposite is where the solicitors' office is today. The long two-storey building in the upper left is W. & A. Smith's boxware factory. In the 1880s this seems to have been known as Smith's Fancy Wood Factory. Opening in 1821, the firm was the village's main souvenir manufacturer for over a hundred years; it received a royal warrant in 1832 to produce razor-sharpening hone stones in fitted boxes. The factory closed in 1937 due to lack of orders and it was demolished in 1963 to make way for the fire station. The showroom is now a pet food store and a commemorative plaque was installed by the Mauchline Ware Society. The making of ware was actually started in Laurencekirk and spread into Ayrshire. In the 1930s and 40s the empty fields in the top left would become the site of council housing on Beechwood Road, Jean Armour Drive and Sunnyside Crescent.

New Road, looking north. The single-storey white house just visible at the top of the right-hand row was a toll house; the first such was further up at the entrance to Netherplace Estate, but was later moved with the opening of New Road in 1820. With road improvements taking place in the 1760s, tolls had to be paid for their maintenance. In 1879 a public roup meeting for the annual sale of tolls was held in the Loudoun Arms Hotel; the minutes recorded: 'nearly all the bars [the moveable toll gates placed across roads to collect payment] have been sold or let but at a reduction. This is owing to the very depressed state of trade, complaints about which were very numerous'. A visitor to Mauchline in 1859 wrote: 'We were followed by the gaze of the whole town: people standing in their doorways, old women popping their heads from the chamber windows, and stalwart men clustering at street corners, merely to stare at our unpretending selves'. The visitors seem to have made a strong impression on the locals!

This view of New Road looks south as far as the Cross and Earl Grey Street, the latter looking much as it is today. The toll house is on the left; when it was in use it had bar gates at which traffic had to stop to pay their dues. Tolls were abolished in 1878 and road maintenance was taken over by Ayr County Council in 1895. The toll house later became a shop owned by J. Baird and Aggie Wilson. W. & A. Smith's office and showroom are adjacent. The cart was probably loaded with finished goods to be taken to the railway station, this occurring twice a day.

These women were staff of the Smith box works; women did the more delicate work, such as putting velvet lining inside boxes, while boys did the varnishing, putting on up to seventeen layers. Male employees were more likely to be machine operators or working to prepare the raw wood, as seen overleaf. In the 1840s the factory was a tourist attraction, one visitor commenting: 'All was so clean and neat and every person appearing to be so well off.' By the early 1900s the workforce numbered 400, the largest of any factory in Ayrshire. A display of fern, tartan and transfer ware at the Great Exhibition of 1851 had increased demand to the extent that two other factories were opened in Castle Street and Barskimming Road. Special wood came on occasions from Kabul, Nineveh and from the tree under which David Livingstone died in Africa. The craftsman responsible for the secret hinges on snuff boxes 'was locked securely away from other staff'. Changes in taste and a fire in 1933 effectively put an end to production. However, Mauchline ware, as it is known as today, is highly prized by collectors.

The National Burns Memorial was opened in May 1898 by J.G.A. Baird MP. It came about as the result of a meeting three years earlier by the Glasgow–Mauchline Society. Architect William Fraser was the designer. The *Ayr Advertiser* reported: 'The first sod was cut by Mr. J. Leiper Gemmill and was thrown high in the air accompanied by the huzzas of the crowd' and that, three weeks later, on the laying of the foundation stone: 'the town was in holiday mood from morn and was literally a mass of bunting. The procession was a mile long and it was estimated that nearly 10,000 people were present.' Six cottages were also opened for farm workers retiring from tied houses and were initially rent free. A further ten were built in 1911 and the last, of a total of 20, opened in 1938. Burns's Mossgiel Farm can be seen in the left background.

This view was taken from the National Burns Memorial. The prefabricated buildings – or 'prefabs' – were built in 1947 to satisfy the great demand for housing after the Second World War. They were quickly erected in pre-made sections as two apartments and occupied extensions of Jean Armour Drive and Sunnyside Crescent. Meant to be only temporary, they lasted until 1970 when – much to the chagrin of many residents – they were finally demolished. They were, however, rehoused in a new council development at Loch Road. In some areas, for example in Cumnock and Stewarton, the prefabs' lifespan was extended by brick and roughcast exteriors and as such are still occupied.

Left: This photograph of Mossgiel Farm shows it more or less as it was when Burns occupied it. This photograph predates 1858 when the walls were raised; they were raised again in 1870 to their present height. The poet and his brother Gilbert sub-leased it from Gavin Hamilton who in turn had a similar lease from the Earl of Loudoun. The brothers' lease began in 1784 on the family's departure from Lochlea and it was here that Burns wrote some of his most important verses and the bulk of those published in the 'Kilmarnock Edition', among them 'To a Mouse', 'The Cottars' Saturday Night' and 'The Holy Fair'. With a thatched roof and access to sleeping quarters by a ladder, the house was far from luxurious. In 1996 and 2009 Mossgiel hosted traditional ploughing matches with Clydesdale horses, attracting over 10,000 spectators on each occasion.

In January 1924 one of the BBC's first outside broadcasts took place of Mossgiel when the Wyllie family, occupants of the farm for almost a century at that time, were interviewed. This was followed later that evening by the live broadcast of the Mauchline Burns Club supper.

Mauchline Colliery opened at Dykefield in the early 1930s. It was owned by Caprington and Auchlochan Collieries Ltd, the director and owner of which lived in Beechgrove House in Mauchline. By 1951, 800 men were employed, 500 of them travelling from as far away as Dreghorn. Buses for Mauchline men on night shift lined up at the Cross around 10 p.m. At that time half a million tons of coal were produced annually. Closure of mining operations came in 1966, with the majority of the workers being transferred to the Barony, Sorn and Lochlea pits, although the plant remained in use to screen coal from the latter two sites. The bing disappeared gradually as its material was used as a base for road building. Today the site is occupied by Ramsay and Jackson's farm implement works and large slabs of granite from Ailsa Craig are also stored there for the Barskimming Road curling stone factory.

This view of the Cross dates to the first week in April 1918 which had been declared Scottish War Service Week; the replica tank was used to publicise the initiative, for which Ayrshire aimed to buy a submarine and several aeroplanes to help the war effort (the result of the effort is unknown). The Mauchline Burns Club built a similar replica and a full-size zig-zag trench for the 2014 Holy Fair festival to mark the centenary of the outbreak of hostilities. In Burns's time the building on the left housed Dr McKenzie's surgery and Merkland's shop. Miss Merkland was one of the poet's 'belles'. Today it is Many Thanks gift shop. The large building opposite was The Place, also known as McShane's building (McShane was possibly a shop owner in the building) and Mauchline House.

The Place stood at the Cross for almost two centuries. It was built by a Mr Gibb, 'a gentleman of rather superior taste', in 1756. However, the Earl of Eglinton was so impressed by it, considering it 'as fine a building as his Castle of Montgomery' (outside Failford), that he purchased it soon after. Its grounds extended up High Street to the summer house at the High Street's junction with Mansefield Road. In 1837 it was cited as having 'Some small pretensions to architectural beauty' but by 1858 circumstances had changed and it was 'a disgrace to the town' (it is unclear when Eglinton sold it on). Before its demolition in the late 1930s, it served as dwelling houses and also held the premises of a grocer and a chip shop. The site then became a car park with steps of rough curling stones. In 1965 a new and enlarged post office and sorting office was built in the space; this lasted until 1992 when it was demolished to make way for a block of housing, a library and council offices. By 2015 the latter two were closed and the premises became a community hub known as Centre Stane.

The Black Bull was originally a coaching inn established in 1756 and is still a working public house today. It was unaffected by the opening up of Earl Grey Street in the 1820s; the street name paid tribute to the politician and tea baron who was closely involved in the voting Reform Act of 1832 and the abolition of slavery. The properties on either side, dating from before 1905, remain largely unchanged. The arch was the entrance to stables, while the giant sized bottles are thought to have been an advertising device for beer. In 1909 a cab business belonging to T. & J. Gibson operated from here. Their advert that year stated they 'Beg to announce that they have removed to more convenient quarters, and cabs, wagonettes, brakes, dog carts, gigs and pony traps always on hire', also 'Trains met in response to letter or wire'.

This view of Earl Grey Street looks very much as it is today with the exception of The Place, now demolished, in the centre. The removal of the Sun Inn allowed the new road a direct route through. The carriages outside the Black Bull were for hire from T. & J. Gibson whose vehicles were stored through the inn's vaulted arch. The building on the left has also since been cleared and is now the site of a filling station. The tall chimney belongs to the boxwork factory further up New Road.

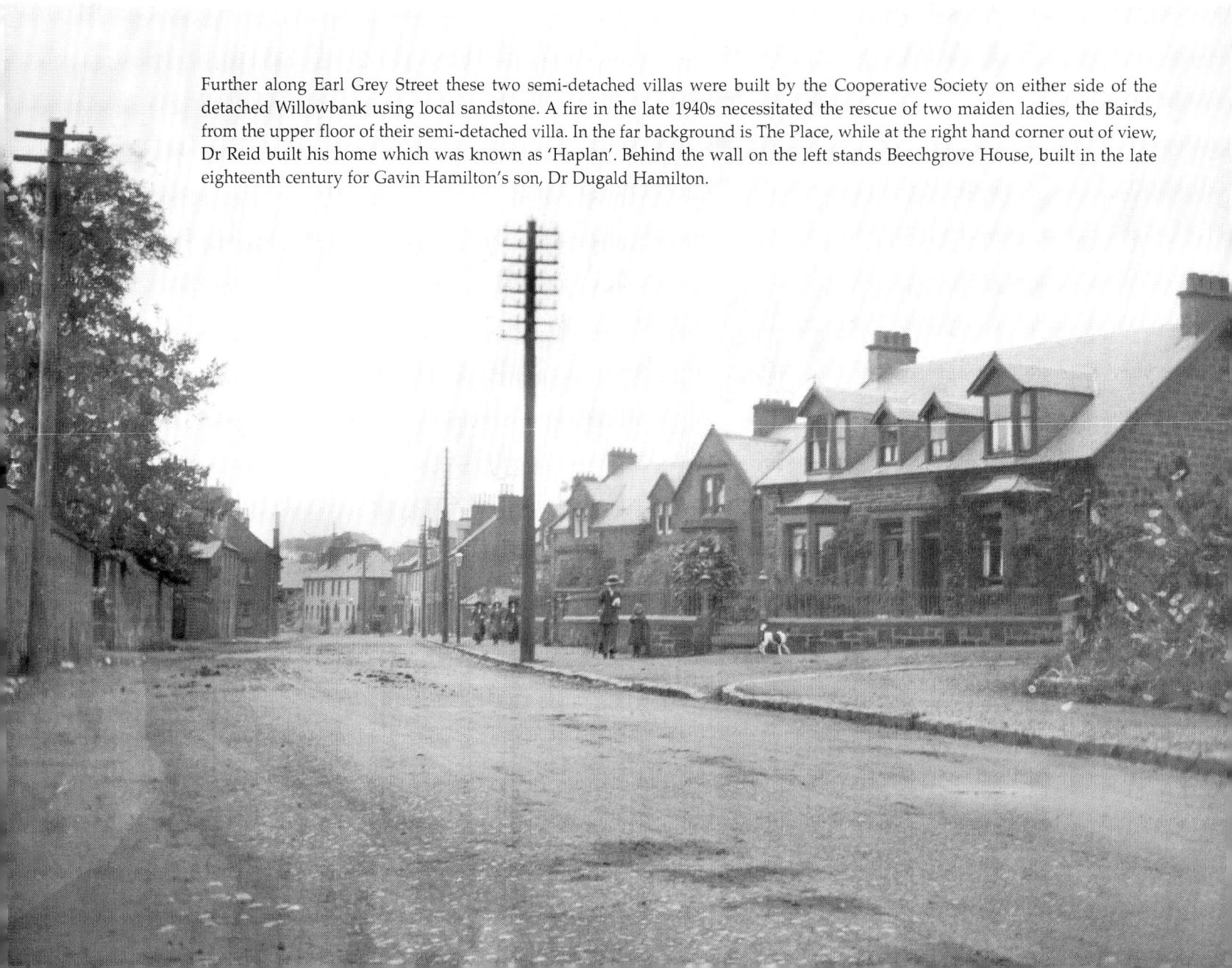

Further along Earl Grey Street these two semi-detached villas were built by the Cooperative Society on either side of the detached Willowbank using local sandstone. A fire in the late 1940s necessitated the rescue of two maiden ladies, the Bairds, from the upper floor of their semi-detached villa. In the far background is The Place, while at the right hand corner out of view, Dr Reid built his home which was known as 'Haplan'. Behind the wall on the left stands Beechgrove House, built in the late eighteenth century for Gavin Hamilton's son, Dr Dugald Hamilton.

Viewfield House, located at the junction of Catrine and Cumnock Roads, was for a long time the only building in this area and it dates from the early 1800s. Gradually other large villas joined it. These, along with other such buildings in the village, often catered for summer visitors, offering either lets or bed and breakfast. A guide book for 1909 asserts 'That as a health resort, Mauchline has few equals'. In the 1930s bungalows were built on the left but, in a sign of the times, they were constructed of brick, not sandstone.

This extension to Ballochmyle House was commissioned in 1887 by its owner, Major General Sir Claud Alexander, on his being created a baronet. It was a Victorian casing of the eighteenth century mansion, which had possibly been by Robert Adam and built for the Whitefords in the 1760s. When the Ayr Bank collapsed in 1772 they suffered financial problems and were forced to sell the property ten years later to the Alexanders. The sister of the new occupant was Wilhelmina Alexander, better known as Burns's 'bonnie lass o' Ballochmyle'. There is a strong possibility the song was recycled for the lady and was actually written for Maria Whiteford. In 1939, as part of the new hospital development, the house served as staff accommodation but dry rot caused its closure for this use. 2005 saw the sale of the whole estate for development as a private gated community, with the mansion house turned into flats.

BALLOCHMYLE HOSPITAL, MAUCHLINE, AYRSHIRE

Emergency Medical Services acquired Ballochmyle Estate in 1939 and had built 32 temporary wards in the prefabricated huts by 1942. Overall there were 1,200 beds and casualties from the Clydebank and Greenock blitzes arrived in large numbers during 1941 and 1942. The Plastic Surgery Unit, which offered help to these victims, soon gained international recognition for its expertise in this field. Later in the war, casualties from the D Day landings were also treated here, as well as Londoners injured by flying bombs. The hospital was taken over by the National Health Service in 1948, serving as the local hospital. It expanded over the next two decades, but with the opening of new facilities at Ayr and Crosshouse and the relocation of specialised units it finally closed in 2000 with the opening of Cumnock Community Hospital. Today the site is a large private housing development.

Above: This area, known as The Haugh, grew up because of its proximity to the River Ayr and the construction of a lade or water channel; a corn mill existed here as early as 1527. Eventually a small village formed as a row of cottages, which had a population of 80 in 1837. The industries included a lint mill, a wool mill, and a curling stone factory, as well as an agricultural implement shop. The woollen mill, the large building in the centre, sent wool for carpet making in Kilmarnock, but burnt down in the 1920s and was not replaced. The cottages themselves were condemned in the 1930s with many of the occupants moving together to the first council houses built on Jean Armour Drive. Around 1913 the curling stone works moved up to the village to occupy an old box works in Barskimming Road. Part of the original building can still be seen as a barn at the Haugh Farm. Further along the river sat Ballochmyle Creamery owned by the McCrone family, one member of which, Guy McCrone, was the author of the *Wax Fruit* trilogy of novels. Later it was taken over by a German firm, Jurgens, the makers of Sea Foam margarine. This closed in 1946, to be taken over by an optical works which in turn closed in 1987. The building is now derelict.

Opposite: The Ballochmyle Viaduct was built for the Glasgow, Paisley, Kilmarnock and Ayr Railway Company, the engineers being Grainger & Miller of Edinburgh. The foundation stone was laid on 5 September 1846, the keystone on 8 April 1847, and the last stone on 12 March 1848. While under construction it was supported by a lattice cradle of Baltic Pine – 1,200 logs, each 14 inches in diameter. These held the masonry until the keystone made it self-supporting. Over 400 men worked on it without fatality; one man fell 100 feet, but was uninjured. On the left is the quarry for the sandstone; however, material for the centre arch came from Dundee as it was harder wearing. The bridge piers are 38 feet wide, while the height from the river bed to the base is 180 feet, making it for a long time the tallest stone arch in the world. The six auxiliary arches have a span of 50 feet. In 1860, the year of the first Open Golf Championships, held at Prestwick, 'Old' Tom Morris stood on the river bed with his club and ball in an attempt to project the ball over the bridge. He failed.

The Barskimming Mill was built beside the River Ayr in 1834, when the lade seen here was widened and deepened. Two water wheels drove six grinding stones, two for shelling oats, two for finishing oat meal and two for flour. The building burned down in 1893 but was rebuilt a year later. It was recognised as one of the largest water-powered mills in Ayrshire. The rivers Ayr and Lugar merge a short distance upstream. In 1966 it became a light engineering factory but was partly demolished in 2009 and fully in 2019. Miller, the owner in Burns's day, had a son who was one of the poet's love rivals in the district.

The first sod of Ballochmyle Quarry in the Haugh Road was cut in 1825 by David Lambie of Catrine who had obtained the lease from Claud Alexander. The site was expanded by 1891 under Marcus Bain and by the turn of the nineteenth century 200 men were employed. The first quarry sat between Haughyet and the railway. Four quarries were developed adjacent to the railway line, going to a depth of 200 feet. A railway siding was installed to cope with as many as 60 wagons a day, with stone being sent as far away as New York where the buildings became known as 'brownstones'. Victoria Cottages, next to the quarries, were built for employees, while in Mauchline itself all new developments, including the Church opened in 1829, used the local stone. In the 1930s, however, bricks and roughcast reduced the demand for the traditional material with the resulting closure of the quarries. Material from local pits and refuse filled in the sites.

The creamery near Barskimming Bridge opened in 1934; in 1950 there were 30 employees largely producing 5 tons of ice cream powder per day. In 1972 expansion in the shape of a new cheese tower was completed (seen here in the centre of the view) and work was extended to packaging. During a two year spell in the 1980s the site was converted to Mozzarella production, but by 1990 it had returned to cheddar and a year later all cheese and butter production ceased and the site continued only as a small pre-packing unit. However, this also ceased with the factory closing completely a year later. It was taken over by a French firm to continue cheese production but in 2007 it transferred work elsewhere and with the departure of First Milk, a company owned by British farmers, in the same year, the factory closed again. The former has been demolished although the other buildings remain. A landscape firm occupies part of the site.

Opposite: The two men are draining whey from the cheese, while the lady is involved in packaging cheese. Both practices were later replaced by more modern technology.

Mauchline Station was opened in 1848 by the Glasgow, Paisley, Kilmarnock and Ayr Railway Company which had to face two huge local construction challenges – Ballochmyle Viaduct and the 680-yards-long Skeoch Tunnel (also known as Mossgiel Tunnel). At the station a footbridge connected the two platforms, the Glasgow line finishing at St Enoch's Station, while the second continued to Ayr and ultimately to Stranraer; this became known as 'the Paddy line' through its connection with Northern Ireland. Early in the twentieth century there were regular day tours for the Burns Trail. These arrived at 10.30, firstly visiting the viaduct, followed by lunch at the Loudoun Arms Hotel, and then visits to various Burns sites, even some fitting in a round of golf or a game of bowls before catching a train at 6.45 p.m. The station also took box ware in its early stages of export and sandstone from the quarries. In 1915 there were 584 train movements through the station and between 30 and 40 men were employed at the station in 1951. However, it closed for freight and passenger traffic in 1965.

This is a view of the Cross and High Street taken from the 90-feet-high church spire. The building in the centre is the post office (under construction) which replaced the one that had been in Loudoun Street in 1965. Formerly this whole site had been a car park, and before that The Place. The post office building was in turn demolished in 1992, ironically returning to its previous home in Loudoun Street (in 2017 this office closed with its inclusion in the Key Store in Kilmarnock Road; the last post master was Jim Robertson). In 1996 a new library was opened on the site with a block of flats adjoining. The library was later moved to the Burns House Museum in 2017 with the premises becoming a community hub.

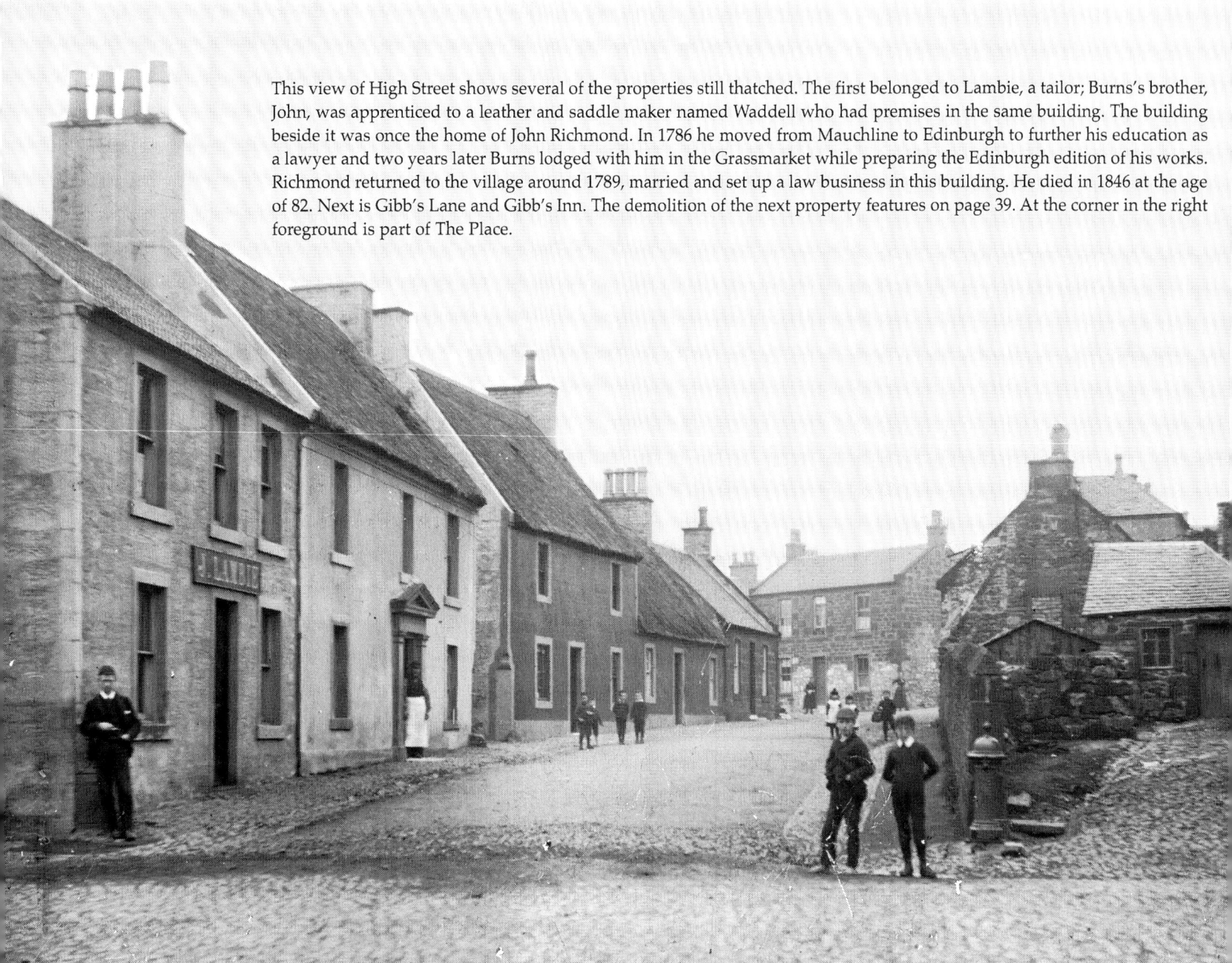

This view of High Street shows several of the properties still thatched. The first belonged to Lambie, a tailor; Burns's brother, John, was apprenticed to a leather and saddle maker named Waddell who had premises in the same building. The building beside it was once the home of John Richmond. In 1786 he moved from Mauchline to Edinburgh to further his education as a lawyer and two years later Burns lodged with him in the Grassmarket while preparing the Edinburgh edition of his works. Richmond returned to the village around 1789, married and set up a law business in this building. He died in 1846 at the age of 82. Next is Gibb's Lane and Gibb's Inn. The demolition of the next property features on page 39. At the corner in the right foreground is part of The Place.

This photograph shows what is likely to be a Sunday school trip going down High Street. The venues for the trips were local farms and estates; novelty races entertained the young folk, who also received bags of foodstuffs donated by the village bakers. The property facing, now Many Thanks, was in Burns's time a shop belonging to the Merkland family, their daughter being one of the poet's 'belles'.

This photograph from 1907 shows work in progress for the building of the two-storey sandstone replacement for No. 7 High Street, next to Gibb's Inn. The two-storey building in the right background still stands, although the thatched houses next door are long gone. The houses along the left are part of Greenhead. The box works chimney is in the centre background. As he lived next door to the new build, John Taylor Gibb photographed various stages of its construction.

Opposite: Gibb's Inn on High Street, which later was known as The Ballochmyle, is now a vets' practice. One of the Gibb family was John Taylor Gibb, the author of *Mauchline, Town and District* (1911), the source of many of the illustrations contained in this book. In Burns's time the inn was occupied by the Findlays whose daughters were famous for their beauty. The inn is also said to have been where, in 1685, General Drummond conducted a summary trial of five Covenanters who were executed further up the street at the Loan. An ancestor of William Fisher, aka Burns's 'Holy Willie', provided the ropes when no-one else would, much to the disgust of the villagers. In the nineteenth century there were thirteen places for alcohol for a population of less than 1,500.

This building in High Street stood opposite Gibb's Inn. The archway served as the rear entrance to the courtyard of The Place. However, it may have pre-dated it by a century as, during the 'Killing times' of the 1680s, Royalist dragoons may have stabled their horses in the sheds through the arch while they themselves were billeted in the nearby inn. It was demolished in the early 1950s and the entrance to Robert Burns Place now stands on the site.

The building in the background was the Thistle Inn on High Street, owned in 1918 by the Train family. In the 1940s it was a general store belonging to Mrs Fairbairn and then, before its demolition, to Mrs Palmer. Pupils on their way to school could buy broken biscuits, cut fruit and cinnamon sticks for smoking. The advert behind the women is for a silent cowboy film *The Black Flag*, released in 1922. However, the womens' clothes look like they come from an earlier era!

This is likely to be a family quartet of the Gibbs in the back garden of their inn sometime before 1914. The property on the left is Burngrange House, which looks more or less the same today. In the 1890s a family dispute brought a curling stone factory to this site separate from the main one at the Haugh. The two amalgamated again in the 1920s at their present site in Barskimming Road. The gas works, the chimney of which can be seen on the right, opened in the late nineteenth century and operated until the 1945 and the introduction that year of a full electricity supply to the town. The agricultural engineering firm Ramsay and Jackson occupied the site of the gas works until its move in 2000 to what had been Mauchline pit. The new housing on the site is Kemp Court, named as a tribute to a long serving local G.P.

At the top of High Street is situated the Loan, the long-standing venue for fairs and markets. In 1847 the New Educational Institute was established here and served as a school until 1888 when, no longer fit for purpose, it was replaced by this new building which could accommodate 474 pupils, both primary and secondary. During the Second World War the school had its own vegetable garden, kept hens and even bees. The Junior Secondary Department closed in 1970 on the opening of Auchinleck Academy, while the building itself was totally renovated in 2007, incorporating a nursery school as well. The front area in its capacity as a public meeting place witnessed the execution of five Covenanters in 1685. The inscribed gravestone was for a long time part of the playground wall until its move to a modern arch in the Loan in front of the school, positioned alongside another stone giving a more legible version of the inscription. A commemorative obelisk was also unveiled in 1885.

The Loan was 'from time immemorial' the public recreation ground for the village with seven annual fairs held there. On race days, always the last Thursday in April, women sold their homemade ales which, according to Adamson, 'would gar your lips stick thegither'. As the location for touring fun fairs and theatres, the public could enjoy such barnstorming productions as 'East Lynn' and 'Maria Martin and the Red Barn'. As can be seen, circuses also visited. The village's water was supplied from an artesian well below the Loan.

Just down from the Cross in Loudoun Street sits the iconic Poosie Nansie's. Its fame arises from Burns's discovery of it when he and two friends, on leaving another nearby hostelry, became aware of music and drunken revelry coming from Poosie's. The noise makers were immortalised in the poet's 'The Jolly Beggars', which, because of its 'licentiousness', was not published in his lifetime. The inn was managed by Black Geordie Gibson, his wife Agnes-Poosie Nansie (hence the name of the establishment) and their daughter Racer Jess. It dates from 1700 and was described by an American visitor in 1857 as 'a two-storey, red-stone, thatched house, looking old, but, by no means venerable'. From 1880 lettering appeared on the gable. An occupant of the building to the right was Tootie McGaun, a contemporary of Burns, and one of the several shoemakers in the village. This was demolished in 1888 to be replaced by a function hall for the inn. The stone the boys are leaning against was to protect the corner from cart axles. An advert in 1909 recommends its 'old brandies and wines for invalids'. In 1910, the shed on the left was replaced by Milne's shop; it later became part of the bar, but was demolished by a car crash in 2014. The thatched roof was changed to slate in 1955 when it was under the ownership of Bill Blake.

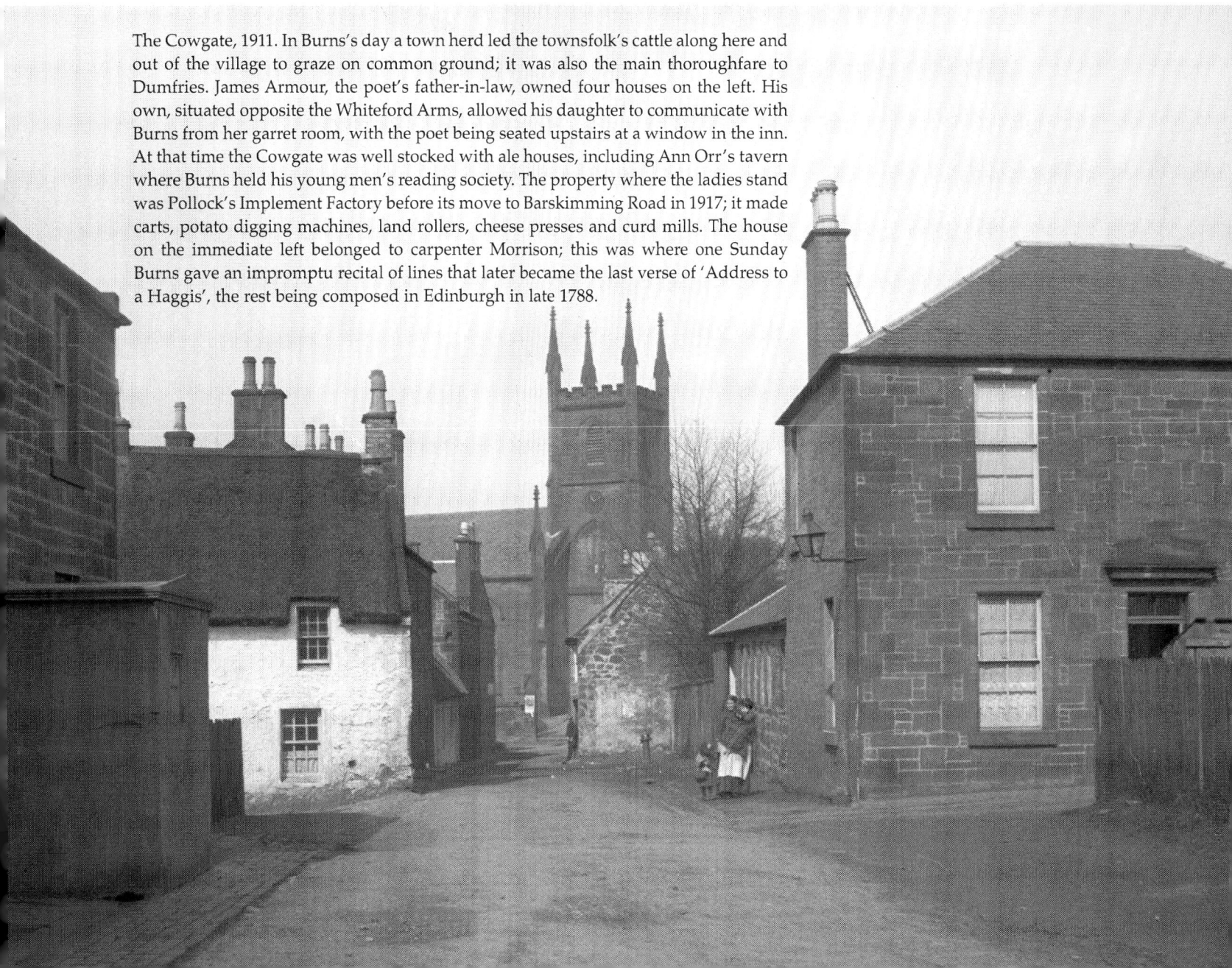

The Cowgate, 1911. In Burns's day a town herd led the townsfolk's cattle along here and out of the village to graze on common ground; it was also the main thoroughfare to Dumfries. James Armour, the poet's father-in-law, owned four houses on the left. His own, situated opposite the Whiteford Arms, allowed his daughter to communicate with Burns from her garret room, with the poet being seated upstairs at a window in the inn. At that time the Cowgate was well stocked with ale houses, including Ann Orr's tavern where Burns held his young men's reading society. The property where the ladies stand was Pollock's Implement Factory before its move to Barskimming Road in 1917; it made carts, potato digging machines, land rollers, cheese presses and curd mills. The house on the immediate left belonged to carpenter Morrison; this was where one Sunday Burns gave an impromptu recital of lines that later became the last verse of 'Address to a Haggis', the rest being composed in Edinburgh in late 1788.

In Loudoun Street the horse and cart are emerging from the Cowgate. The site of The Whiteford Arms on the corner had by this time been taken by the Cooperative grocery store on the left which, on its expansion further down the street, became a boot and shoe store. The original building was frequented by Burns and his trio of friends and here the group held its 'Court of Equity', enquiring satirically into local sexual misdemeanours. The plaque on the chimney breast commemorating the original building is now on the gable end. In 1956 the property behind the man with the hat and handcart opened as a branch of the Bank of Scotland with Archie McEwan as manager; it closed in 1997. The arch further down the street was the entrance to the Abbey Church. The single storey building beyond it was replaced by a two-storey in 1900 as Blair's bakery.

The Mauchline Cooperative Society was founded in 1863 with this shop (earlier and later facades of the same premises are seen here) opening on the site of the Whiteford Arms in 1866. In 1928 properties between the church and the entrance to Gavin Hamilton's house were demolished and opened as a Cooperative grocery, with its own bakery in the yard behind. This was a period of considerable Cooperative expansion under the management of Roderick Cameron. The floor above the grocery sold white electrical goods, while a butcher's was next door on the ground floor. Across the road there were two shops - tobacconist and confectioner with the Jean Armour function suite above. Up in Earl Grey Street, one premises specialised in TV and audio goods while further along was a gents' outfitters.

As the Cooperative expanded its properties, it also catered for customers in its mobile vans, this one selling the firm's own baking goods. Until 1952 horse-drawn carts fulfilled the same purpose. One Co-op horse, an ex-circus animal, danced to any radio music coming from open windows; another knew houses where it would be fed by housewives and made a quick trot there with lady customers following on behind. When mobile vans took over there were three baker vans, two butcher vans, a coal lorry and two mobile shops for rural areas. When the Scottish Cooperative Wholesale Society took over the Cooperative in 1968, they withdrew all the vans, much to the protest of customers and staff.

This view of Loudoun Street looking east dates from before 1910; however, with the exception of the single-storey building (now two storeys), it looks very much the same today. In part of the main block in the centre was Blair's bakery, where a special treat on a Saturday evening pre-1914 would be to buy seven pies for the equivalent in today's money of just five pence. In the 1930s the shop on the right became the premises of the Mauchline Press, a printing business know locally as the 'printer's', which was owned by Willie Whitelaw and closed in 2003. It is now a private house. The gap further up was soon to become the entrance to the newly built Abbey Church. The lady in the apron standing at the entrance to the Castle is likely to have been a servant there.

Opposite: This house off Loudoun Street was owned by the Earl of Loudoun and leased to Gavin Hamilton, lawyer, friend and patron of Robert Burns. The poet leased Mossgiel Farm from Hamilton and in turn dedicated the 'Kilmarnock Edition' of his poetry to him. A free thinker, Hamilton was frequently in dispute with the kirk session, as described in Burns's 'Holy Willie's Prayer'. Highland Mary Campbell was nurse maid to the family. In 1788 Burns and Jean Armour were officially married in the property by a Sorn J.P. The west wing was added as a nursery by Hamilton's son. The adjacent tower, known locally as the Castle, was in fact part of a monastic grange.

A view from outside the Loudoun Arms Hotel, taken from the corner with Barskimming Road. In 1909 the hotel (now the Fairburn) advertised its 'Splendid cuisine and liquors of the highest quality', a contrast with 60 years earlier when Mrs Nathaniel Hawthorne had to be content with 'a sheep's head and broth' when she stayed there overnight. A writer in 1879 recorded of Mauchline, 'today the sound of the shuttle is no longer heard; the weaving of cotton once formed the chief support of the inhabitants' but Mrs Hawthorn confirmed this much earlier: 'Its chief business appears to be the manufacture of snuff boxes'. The shell of the properties on the right are still to be seen today. At the very foot, again on the right, stands Campbell House with the inscription above the doorway 'circa 1783'.

The Loudoun Arms Hotel, formerly McClelland's Inn and today the Fairburn, was a stopping-off place to change coach horses. It was here Burns set up a reading group to discuss and exchange books. One James Humphrey, described by the poet as 'a bletherin' bitch', unashamedly cashed in on the poet's reputation by begging from passengers of the coaches. Behind the horses is the Loudoun Spout, whose source is Ayrshire's oldest artesian well. It was renovated in 2000 as a Millennium project. This photograph was taken in 1912 with a member of the Hamilton–Campbell family inspecting a group of Ayrshire Yeomanry cavalry, which had been established in 1796. The single-storey houses were replaced by council houses in the 1960s while the arch was opened in the nineteenth century as an entrance to Netherplace House.

The Abbey Kirk was opened with full Masonic honours in 1884 and, after varied usage, was demolished in 1969. By 1900 the village had two United Free churches, the Walker Memorial and the Abbey; a union took place in 1925 with the Walker Memorial being renamed the North Church. For some time the Abbey was used as the Sunday school building and as a session meeting place. However, in 1940 the building was converted into a cinema by John Lawrence, to be operated by his son Robert. The programme changed three times a week with a matinee and two performances on a Saturday. A common event for the matinee was when boys from the approved Catholic school at Barskimming were marched up in their black rain coats and tackety boots to sit as a group at the back of the cinema. After a period as a bingo hall, it closed in 1963, when it was taken over as a builders' yard by Thomas Findlay and Sons, who subsequently sold it to a similar firm, Robison and Davidson. It was closed down in the 1980s and demolished around 2000, with the social housing of Curling Stone Place replacing it.

The first reference to Netherplace House was in 1569 when Mungo Campbell gave his brother 'a disposition for lands now called Netherplace'. The older part of the house was recorded in 1641 and was considerably extended in the early nineteenth century. In Burns's day a main road passed its frontage. When the Campbells were succeeded by the Hamilton–Campbells in the 1850s, the imposing new frontage was added. On a son being awarded the VC for his bravery at Sebastopol during the Crimea War, there was a firework display and three cannons were fired. The property remained in the family until 1954, when it was purchased by Sir Claud Alexander. However, when Sir Claud realised the probable cost of renovation, he sold it to the building firm MacTaggart and Mickel, who demolished the mansion and developed the estate for private housing.

Wilson Place on the left, now demolished, was in Barskimming Road. Behind it was (and is) the curling stone factory. Another boxware factory, belonging to Wilson, Amphlet and Davidson's boxware factory, having moved from Castle Street in 1859, had stood on the site but in 1885 the building was sold to their Smith competitors who needed to expand. In 1901 it was sold again to Andrew Kay & Co., who moved their curling stone manufacturing from The Haugh and it is still used for this today. The houses on the right are still occupied.

The curling stone factory started at The Haugh in 1851 where the lade gave easy access to water power. The original 'ice stone mill' can still be seen at the roadside of the Haugh Farm. Around 1910 Andrew Kay and Company's works moved up to their present location in Barskimming Road. Currently 45 stones weighing 40 pounds are produced per week by ten craftsmen. The granite is transported from Ailsa Craig at intervals depending on demand and stored locally. The firm, still family owned, has also branched into the souvenir trade with miniature stones and even jewellery. The Olympics committee restored curling to its roster of recognised sports in 1998 and with the 2022 Winter Olympics being held in China indications are the output will need to double to cope with projected demand.

Back cover: This rear view of Gavin Hamilton's house and the adjacent Castle was taken before the construction of the church hall in 1895 (it would stand in the foreground of this view). A square of houses including Morton's Inn had occupied the site, long before this photograph was taken, the daughter of the inn owner being one of Burns's 'belles'. In 1165 Walter, High Steward of Scotland, granted these lands to the monks of Melrose as a grange rather than a monastery. The tower was erected by Abbot Hunter around 1450; this did not stand alone, but was part of a complex of buildings including the church which Burns later attended. During Covenanter times, the castle was used to house prisoners. Hamilton's house was built in the late seventeenth century with the wing on the right being later added by Dr Hamilton, Gavin's son.

Old Mauchline

Ian Lyell

Published by:
Stenlake Publishing Limited
54–58 Mill Square, Catrine,
Ayrshire, KA5 6RD.
01290 551122
www.stenlake.co.uk

£11.95

ISBN 9781840338683